THE PARTITION PRINCIPLE:
Remapping Quebec
After Separation

The Partition Principle:
Remapping Quebec after Separation

Trevor McAlpine

ECW PRESS

CANADIAN CATALOGUING IN PUBLICATION DATA

McAlpine, Trevor,
The partition principle : remapping Quebec after separation

ISBN 1-55022-291-0

1. Quebec (Province) – History – Autonomy and
independence movements. 2. Quebec (Province) –
Politics and government – 1995- 3. Canada –
Politics and government – 1993- 4. Partition,
Territorial.   1. Title.

FC2926.9.S4M32 1996   971.4'04   C96-990055-4
F1053.2.M321996

Cover photo by Shaun Best, courtesy Reuters (Archive Photos).

Design and imaging by ECW Type & Art, Oakville, Ontario.
Printed by Imprimerie Québecor L'Eclaireur, Beauceville, Québec.

Distributed in Canada by General Distribution Services,
30 Lesmill Road, Don Mills, Ontario M3B 2T6.

www.ecw.ca/press

Published by ECW PRESS,
2120 Queen Street East, Suite 200,
Toronto, Ontario M4E 1E2.

TABLE OF CONTENTS

ACKNOWLEDGEMENTS

Authors often say that their books would not have been possible without the dedicated help of others. It is true. Special thanks go to Brent Tyler, former spokesman for the Special Committee on Canadian Unity, for his unflinching help in framing the main issues, and to Keith Henderson, leader of the Equality Party, for his lessons about partition's history and willingness to supply important documentation.

Many thanks go to all who reviewed my manuscript, especially Scott Reid and Stephen Scott for their comments, which helped immeasurably. Kudos to the capable staff at ECW who brooked my many questions and missed deadlines; likewise, to the people at PBA for allowing me a flexible working arrangement, even when it inconvenienced them.

Guy Bertrand must also be thanked for his courageous stand against Quebec's UDI attempts. His sacrifice reminded me that staying Canadian is not a given; it requires constant vigilance. "Protégera nos foyers et nos droits / We stand on guard for thee" are not just idle words. My final thank-you is to my family, who have suffered me while I wrote.

Preface

Quebec cannot secede from Canada and expect to retain its present borders. This is the position of those who advocate partition, and it is the focus of this book. I do not attempt to analyse the Quebec separatist movement here, nor do I explore what, if any, modifications are needed to the Canadian constitution or governmental administrative arrangements to "renew federalism."

In exploring the partition option, this book neither seeks to legitimize brinkmanship games nor puts forth a call to arms. It simply examines partition as plan B, to be invoked only if the government of Quebec actively pursues the secessionist option, either by negotiating with, or unilaterally seceding from, Canada. But if partition is to be enacted it must be debated now, while we still have both the time and the energy to do so. The eve of a referendum or an election is a poor time to begin exploring options for the future of this country.

As a reader, I am always as curious to know *why* an author has chosen to write a given book as I am about its contents. I wrote this book because the partition issue has the potential to affect, permanently and profoundly, the lives of all Canadians. For too long, the issues that bear upon the future of Quebec within Canada have been the exclusive province of political elites. The partitionist movement heralds the end of this monopoly: it is primarily a grass-roots initiative fuelled by people and organizations who are tired of being used as pawns in the separation game, tired of seeing certain fundamental hypocrisies in the Quebec nationalist agenda persistently ignored. My purpose is to help explain and give voice to some of the issues that define this movement.

There is still much confusion surrounding partition in the public eye and in the media: the federal government has yet to demonstrate true leadership in the context of this issue; the media, the daily stream of newspaper reports and television newscasts, keep us informed about the statements and actions of the proponents of partition, but generally fail to provide synthesis, analysis. The concept of partition as it applies to the current situation in Quebec needs to be defined, examined, and tested, and this book constitutes my attempt to respond to that need.

Introduction

Sectioning off territory from what is today recognized as the province of Quebec as part of the terms of the agreement that would allow the province to secede legally from the Canadian federation is currently described as *partition*. For most concerned individuals, partition, thus understood, is part of plan B — a strategy to be enacted only if all other strategies to keep Canada together prove unsuccessful. Advocates of this plan are, first and foremost, advocates of Canadian unity. But, as with all contingency plans, a policy must be formulated before crisis is upon us. Once a partition policy stands, it will act as a sobering reminder that if Quebec secedes from Canada, the price may be much higher than Quebec nationalists claim.

The idea of partitioning the seceding state of Quebec is still a relatively new one. Former prime minister Pierre Trudeau declared in the late 1970s that "If Canada is divisible, Quebec should be divisible too."[1]

---

1 Qtd. in William F. Shaw and Lionel Albert, *Partition: The Price of Quebec's Independence* (Montreal: Thornhill, 1980) 16.

In 1980, Lionel Albert and William F. Shaw published *Partition: The Price of Quebec's Independence*, based on their work with the Preparatory Committee for an Eleventh Province. In it, they argue that Quebec cannot reasonably expect to secede with its borders intact, and they redraw the province's borders based on historical evidence of land ownership.

Over the next decade and a half, these voices were joined by others. In 1991, David Varty's *Who Gets Ungava?* appeared; it explains why the territories that were added to Quebec in 1898 and 1912 should revert back to Canada in the event of Quebec's separation. In the same year, York University hosted a symposium on partition. Scott Reid's *Canada Remapped: How the Partition of Quebec Will Reshape the Nation* came out in 1992, and served to popularize the idea that, by establishing the new boundaries of an independent state of Quebec according to certain democratic procedures, we can reduce the risk of violence. The Equality Party of Quebec raised the issue of partition during the 1994 provincial election, and both the Equality Party and the Special Committee for Canadian Unity filed briefs on the question with the Quebec government's Sovereignty Commission in early 1995.

For many people, though, the idea of partition was either unknown or undefined as of the summer of 1995. It should have been raised then, during the campaign leading up to Quebec's 30 October 1995 referendum on sovereignty, giving voters the opportunity to assess fully the steep price of separation; but this did not occur. The official federalist "no" committee, created in accord with Quebec's referendum law and run by the Quebec Liberal Party, refused to advance the partition argument itself and chose not to provide other groups with the funding necessary to do so. This specifically targeted the Special Committee for Canadian Unity, which was formed in 1994 (the Equality Party was one of its founding members) to fight secession by using arguments, such as those concerning partition, that diverged from the Quebec Liberal Party program. Federalist politicians and the media (with the notable exception of William Johnson, columnist for the Montreal *Gazette*) proved generally reluctant to address the issue; it was often portrayed as an extremist notion that would engender social unrest.

The architects of federalist strategy during the referendum campaign were at a loss to explain why the "no" side experienced a drastic erosion in support as the vote drew near: "no" finally prevailed over "yes" by a mere fifty-five thousand ballots. The closeness of the result and the revelation that then premier Jacques Parizeau had taped a victory speech before those results were known — a speech that left no doubt about his government's determination to take Quebec out of Canada as rapidly as possible — came as a shock to many. The partitionist option was becoming harder to ignore.

A little-advertised public rally was held at McGill University's moot court on 21 January 1996 to address the illegality of a unilateral declaration of independence (UDI), the concept of partition, and other issues. It drew an audience of twelve hundred. Hundreds more had to be turned away. Partition had entered the mainstream of political debate.

On 27 January 1996, just six days after the rally at the moot court, Stéphane Dion, the Université de Montréal political-science professor who had just been appointed federal intergovernmental affairs minister, prompted a flurry of media attention by raising the notion of partition publicly: "You can't consider Canada divisible but the territory of Quebec sacred," he stated.[1] Dion had launched the idea of partition within the governmental establishment, and others ran with it. "It's the logical answer," said Prime Minister Jean Chrétien on 30 January 1996: "If Canada is divisible, Quebec is divisible."[2] With these words, the prime minister finally moved the idea of partition from the margins of political thought to its centre and tacitly acknowledged its grass-roots validity.

Progressive Conservative leader Jean Charest, considered by many to be the best spokesman for a strong Quebec in a united Canada during the 1995 referendum campaign, remarked: "If [separatists] have a right to dissent they can't deny the right of dissent to others. . . . It's part of the black hole they would be walking into if ever there were a Yes vote."[3] The leader of

1   Bob Cox, "Partition after Separation OK: Dion," *Gazette* 27 Jan. 1996: A1.

2   Paul Wells, "Chrétien, Ministers See Logic of Partitioning," *Gazette* 30 Jan. 1996: A1.

3   "Quebec Probably Is Divisible: Charest," *Gazette* 29 Jan. 1995: A5.

Quebec's official opposition, Liberal Daniel Johnson, said: "Nobody can guarantee that on an international level if Quebec secedes from Canada everything will stay the way it is today . . . nobody can offer any guarantees about territory, about citizenship. It is all up in the air."[1]

Lucien Bouchard, then premier-designate of Quebec, replied to Dion's remarks by declaring: "I think deeply and intensely that in Quebec we are a people, we are a nation and as a nation we have a fundamental right to keep, maintain and protect our territory. . . . Canada is divisible because Canada is not a real country. There are two people, two nations, and two territories — and this one is ours."[2] The double standard was starkly revealed. Secessionists believe that Quebecers have the collective right to partition Canada, but no group has the right to partition Quebec. Canadians outside of Quebec are not permitted to have a say in the choice of Quebecers, and if Quebecers decide to leave Canada, then they will do so taking all of their territory with them.

The increased attention given to partition had some negative repercussions. There was a concerted effort by Quebec nationalists to associate the notion with violence, thereby discrediting it. Daniel Johnson quickly reverted back to his party's official line, saying that Quebec's borders were not subject to change in

---

[1] "Quebec Probably Is Divisible."

[2] Philip Authier, "Bouchard Says No to Partition," *Gazette* 28 Jan. 1996: A1–A2.

the event of secession. After analysing only the most limited partition scenario — the creation of an eleventh province from the western end of the island of Montreal — many columnists attacked partition as unworkable and denounced it as a divisive concept. (They seemed to overlook the powerfully divisive effect of the Quebec government's separation agenda.) *La Presse* columnist Lysiane Gagnon, in a piece called "Over Our Dead Bodies!", almost guaranteed that the very idea of partition would drive francophones to violence.[1]

Since the initial comments were made, the partition issue has evolved, becoming even more emotionally charged — as charged as the issue of separation itself. In fact, Quebec separatists are the *original* partitionists: they seek to partition Canada. After decades of developing the separatist option largely unimpeded by the conflicting claims of other groups, they now find themselves in the uncomfortable position of having to explain why no portion of the province can elect to remain Canadian if Quebec achieves independence. Bouchard's answer — "because Canada is not a real country" — falls pathetically short as an explanation. During the referendum campaign, Chantal Hébert, Ottawa bureau chief for *La Presse*, commented:

> There are issues that the Bloc [Québécois] doesn't want to raise in the house despite the fact

---

1 Lysiane Gagnon, "Over Our Dead Bodies!", *La Presse* 23 Jan. 1996: B3.

that they would be newsy. When the External Affairs Minister, André Ouellet, for instance, went into Quebec this week and mentioned that Quebec's territory may not be whole if it separated, it could be divided as much as Canada's territory could be divided, the Bloc was reluctant to raise the issue in the house because that is exactly the type of issue that its strategists figure scare voters away from the yes side. So they have to drop all of those issues that are bound to raise doubts about the tomorrows of a yes.[1]

People who worry that the partition option, by its very nature, will polarize views and threaten social peace miss the point. The threat does not originate with those who support the partitioning of a seceding Quebec: it has come, for many years, from those who would partition Canada. Social peace is endangered primarily by those who supported holding two referendums on sovereignty and would now welcome a third. For them, the emotional and financial toll these votes have taken is an acceptable price to pay for the chance of making their dream of a new country a reality.

---

[1] "Why the Bloc Is Reluctant to Discuss Territory," political panel, CBC Newsworld, Toronto, 21 Sept. 1995.

Why Now?
The Purposes and Goals
of an Urgent Debate

Many Canadians and Quebecers were convinced that separation would never happen. Federalists — the "no" side — were sure of victory up until the final stretch of the 1995 referendum campaign, with polls reporting that only about thirty-five percent of voters supported the "yes" side. Then Lucien Bouchard, leader, at that time, of the Bloc Québécois (the official opposition in Parliament after the 1993 federal election), was asked to be Quebec's chief negotiator with Canada in the event that the secessionists won. Bouchard dismissed any reference to the potential economic results of secession;[1] instead, he concentrated on emotional appeals. "L'effet Bouchard" propelled the separatists to within fifty-five thousand votes of victory, or just under 1.2 percent of all the votes cast in the referendum.

---

[1] See, for example, Philip Authier, "Bouchard Drops Studies: Le Hir's Work Part of 'Previous' Campaign," *Gazette* 11 Oct. 1995: A1, A10.

Both Bouchard and Jacques Parizeau, then premier of Quebec and leader of the Parti Québécois, advocated the idea that Quebec could secede on its own terms. A separate Quebec, they maintained, would use the Canadian dollar, enter NAFTA, retain all of its territory, and pay Canada whatever share of the national debt that it pleased. No one could stop Quebec from leaving Canada on Quebec's terms, and no one could alter Quebec's borders. They even declared that the province could apply pressure tactics, such as withholding debt payments, to force Canada to accept Quebec's terms and timetables.

With Bill 1, the Act Respecting the Future of Quebec (tabled by Parizeau on 7 September 1995), the separatists established a one-year grace period during which all terms of separation were to be negotiated with Canada. This grace period could be unilaterally terminated if Quebec felt that the desired results were not being achieved, and Quebec would be free to make a UDI. They reassured Quebecers that separation would entail no major disruptions either in Quebec or the rest of Canada.

Federalist strategists convinced many that all Canada needed to do was to ensure that Quebecers felt welcome within the federation. The concept of separation was unthinkable and the less said about such hypothetical situations the better. Aside from advancing economic arguments on the cost of separation, the federal government never challenged separatist claims that separation would be easy, legal, and total. In fact, it took a private citizen, Quebec City lawyer Guy

Bertrand, to mount a legal challenge to the Quebec government's draft bill on sovereignty. Only in September of 1996 did the federal government finally decide to ask the Supreme Court of Canada to determine whether a UDI is legal under the Canadian constitution and international law.

For years, the separatist camp has defined the terms of the debate and used subtle forms of persuasion and emotional blackmail to make federalists accept that separation is reasonable and legal — even if achieved by means of a UDI. The federal government has responded to these tactics with a dangerous complacency. The need to structure a debate on the real issues that would affect Quebec and Canada in the event of separation while there is still time has become desperate. Fortunately, grass-roots pressure to adopt a firm position has begun to wear on the federal government, and Bertrand has convinced Ottawa to help him argue before the courts that the Canadian constitution takes precedence over any assumed right of sovereignty, and thus to counter directly the Quebec government's claim that the democratic will of the people is paramount. Any federalist complacency towards the notion of partition must be overcome as well. Partition must be recognized as an integral aspect of the debate about Canada's future.

Quebecers and Canadians in general are suffering from the emotional fatigue brought on by constant exposure to the Quebec question. We have been forcibly drawn into major debates, ruthlessly polled, and subjected to much aggressive campaigning. Within a few years we have witnessed Meech Lake (from 1987 to 1990), the Charlottetown Accord (1992), a federal election (1993), a Quebec provincial election (1994), a referendum on sovereignty (1995), the ascension of Lucien Bouchard to the premiership of Quebec and leadership of the Parti Québécois (1996), and the by-elections of Jean Chrétien's two Quebec cabinet stars, Stéphane Dion and Pierre Pettigrew (1996).

Although our fatigue is understandable, succumbing to it is perilous. The concept of separation has become an important part of the Canadian political landscape because, over the years, its tireless proponents have kept it in the public eye. If federalists do not, with equal energy, define, promote, and analyse the concept of partition as part of a planned response to secession, it will fade from view, and its potential advantages will be lost. If — simply by virtue of the familiarity it would take on if debate is kept alive — partition becomes entrenched in public consciousness, just as separatism has become entrenched over the last forty years, it will no longer seem reactionary or inappropriate; partition will seem as legitimate as any other factor in the secession debate.

There is a supreme irony to the fact that the majority of separatists and a number of Quebec federalists — all of whom, of course, believe themselves to be democratic — consider any discussion of partition to be heresy. If we even entertain the notion, they warn, we will all be doomed to social unrest. They often urge Quebecers to work on "positive" solutions to the problem that confronts us — solutions that will not divide and polarize. While such solutions are always desirable, these "positive thinkers" manage to ignore the fact that it is the separatists who have consistently advocated divisive solutions to the challenges facing Canada, and who rely on polarization to achieve their ends. The exchange of ideas is the cornerstone of democracy; anything that prevents such exchange negates democracy. No one would seriously advocate that we ban all discussion of separation. The partition movement deals with verifiable historical, political, legal, and social facts as much as it does with people's desire to remain Canadian; it does not entail hate-mongering or negative solutions. Partition is a viable and legitimate option, and therefore partitionists must be permitted to add their voices to the clamour of the ongoing democratic debate that feeds our society.

If partition is debated now, it may check the growing attraction to the idea of separation as a quick fix for what ails Quebec. It may serve to remind Canadians living outside Quebec that there are many Quebecers who refuse to be sacrificed on the altar of constitutional peace; partitionists, for the most part, do not endorse the idea that the rest of Canada should "just let Quebec go." The debate will perhaps also prompt some Quebec nationalists to look at the arguments they use to justify secession from the viewpoint of those negatively affected by them.

One of the debate's greatest benefits may be its ability to expose as a lie the idea that a separate Quebec will still, somehow, be a part of Canada. It also gives beleaguered federalists fuel in their ideological struggle with blue-sky separatists. Separation cannot be painless. Separation has repercussions, and is not an end in itself. The concept of cutting Canada into pieces fills Canadians with dread; the possibility that Quebec will be divided into two or more sections frightens and appals Quebec nationalists. It undermines the sense of identity that derives from having a homeland, and damages pride. Partition mirrors the anguish felt for years by federalists threatened with the breakup of Canada. If partitioning Canada would be so painless, why do nationalists dread the partitioning of Quebec? It is, quite simply, the height of folly not to recognize that carving any territory out of Canada or Quebec would lead to economic hardship, displacement, and hard feelings. That is why most partitionists see their option as part of plan B, to be pursued only if all appropriate measures to keep Quebec within the Canadian federation have failed.

Tackling the issue of partition now, within the context of the secessionist agenda, helps Quebecers to bring their priorities into focus. Federalists worry and secessionists hope that the spectre of partition will drive soft nationalists into the separatist camp. Since the vast majority of "yes" voters are francophone, the assumption is that following a secessionist referendum victory, if partition is put to a further vote, francophones will opt en masse to reject it and to stay in the new state of Quebec, even if they had initially preferred to remain Canadian. This has not been proven. In fact, a CROP poll conducted after the 1995 referendum — based on the question "Knowing that the regions that vote 'no' would not be part of Quebec and would stay with Canada, would you vote 'yes' or 'no' to sovereignty?" — showed a drop of three percent in "yes" voters.[1] These results demonstrate that a number of Quebecers are making hard decisions about their future and facing the sacrifices separation would inevitably entail head on.

Talk of secession is divisive. Many French-Canadians in Quebec feel caught between a rock and a hard place. They have a strong attachment to the one Canadian province where the French language is predominant, yet are reluctant to forego the formidable benefits of Canadian citizenship and the sense of identity it confers. The debate over separation polarizes them; it forces them to make a difficult choice, one that can divide families and destroy friendships. Serious attention must be paid to the situation of these people as solutions to the national-unity conundrum are sought.

Their concerns must be addressed within the partition debate now and as it develops. North America has risen before them as a vast sea of English- and Spanish-speaking peoples that threatens the very survival of their francophone culture. Partitionists must assure French Canadian federalists that their language and culture will have the means to thrive within a post-secession partitioned political landscape. The Equality Party and the Special Committee for Canadian Unity, whose members are articulate defenders of the

---

1 Qtd. in "Partition: Les Québécois Disent Non!" *L'actualité* 15 May 1996: 39. Author's translation.

partition option, have already taken the positive step of declaring that partitioned federalist territory should be made officially bilingual.

Premier Bouchard frequently states that he would prefer to focus not on the question of separation and partition but on the real issues, as he sees them: salvaging Quebec's economy and reducing its debt load. What he fails to see is that partition is perceived by many as a very real issue, a fundamental issue. The federal government, in turn, has been slow to recognize the urgent need to address the issue of partition. Partitionists believe that Canadians should be told the unvarnished truth about secession: if backed into a corner — if Quebec makes a UDI — Canada will in all probability exercise its basic rights as a sovereign state and act decisively to defend both its territory against illegal seizure and its citizens against any infringement of their rights. It is imperative that the separatist option be pursued within the framework of the Canadian constitution. If it is not, a legal vacuum will be created in which Canada may agree to let Quebec go, but it can do so only after it secures the rights of those who wish to remain its citizens.

Many Quebec nationalists claim the right to remove their province from the federation without recourse to due constitutional process, yet categorically deny the right of others to remain in Canada or break away from an independent Quebec. The hypocrisy of such a position should have provoked the media and intelligentsia to voluble dissent. Bouchard's government and its supporters should be facing a constant barrage of questions and demands for clarification. That this has not happened is indicative of how dysfunctional public debate in the province has become.

Canada is a sovereign state. Its jurisdiction within its borders is absolute and recognized under international law. As such, it has the right and the obligation to defend its interests from any who threaten it, whether externally or internally. Canada must take action to reduce the uncertainty under which its citizens are living. The threat of separation bears upon our most fundamental concerns: it erodes the quality of our lives by fuelling anxieties about the stability of our jobs and investments, and, as a consequence, the stability of home and family; it causes us to fear for something we have long taken for granted — our citizenship. Partition may be our best means of defence, and the time has come to deploy it.

The Substance
of Partition:
Issues That
Structure the Debate

The partition movement embraces a compendium of issues. It is a complex response to a complex problem, and its advocates, although united in their loyalty to Canada and their determination to preserve its integrity first and foremost, represent a spectrum of concerns and backgrounds. In this section, I will review some of the issues on which partition is founded.

The Constitution

The first is the issue of the constitution, the fundamental law of the land from which all other laws and institutions derive their legitimacy. Constitutional democracies such as Canada operate according to the rule-of-law principle. This dictates that individuals and governments must act within the limits of specified, impartially administered, and codified laws. We may elect representatives who then vote to alter laws according to established procedures. The constitution is protected from being dismantled by such procedures; to prevent it from being changed by simple majority votes, it has been equipped with an amending formula. There is no existing mechanism in the Canadian constitution that allows for a province to leave the federation: in order for Quebec to secede legally from Canada, a constitutional amendment is required. A referendum is *not* a substitute for a constitutional amendment. It is a tool that a government may employ to obtain a direct reading of public opinion, but the results cannot legally bind it to a particular course of action.

Secessionists have claimed that there is no higher law than the democratic will of the people. They insist that if a constitution were to block the democratically indicated aspirations of its subjects, it would be a case of "extreme justice, extreme injustice": an injustice perpetrated by an excessively rigorous application of the law. On the strength of such arguments, they have attracted many supporters and fostered a sense of the inevitability of separation that has led to its acceptance in many sectors. Their approach, however, is simply not valid. The rule of law must be upheld.

One of the basic elements of this rule is the series of laws that prohibit any majority from oppressing any minority, regardless of the issue that divides them. These laws are an essential deterrent to civil strife. Our constitution was established with a purposefully stringent amending formula so that all citizens may enjoy permanence and security as governments come and go. The rule of law is not merely a clever argument designed to annoy separatists.

Because Quebec did not sign the 1982 Canada Act repatriating the constitution, many separatists have reasoned, the province need not be bound by it. This is a false argument: the Supreme Court of Canada has already determined that since ninety percent of the provinces signed the constitution, it is now legal and applicable to all Canadians. And even if Quebec was bound only by the original 1867 British North America Act, it still could not leave Canada at will. In most cases, amendments to the BNA Act had to be passed by the British Parliament; the act was one of its instruments. But twice before provinces attempting to separate from their countries were denied permission to do so by the British Parliament because the requests came from the provinces themselves, and not from the federal governments of the countries involved.[1]

Thus, even if Canada had not repatriated the constitution in 1982, Quebec would still have been obliged to negotiate with Canada to obtain its autonomy. If the Quebec government had been given a clear mandate by the people of Quebec to negotiate separation, then

---

1 Nova Scotia attempted to secede from Canada in 1868; Western Australia from the Commonwealth in 1933–34. In both cases, voters had approved the secession via a petition or referendum by a clear majority. See Grand Council of the Crees, *Sovereign Injustice: Forcible Inclusion of the James Bay Crees and Cree Territory into a Sovereign Quebec* (Nemaska, QC: Grand Council of the Crees, 1995) 333n1,167, n1,168.

Canada, in the process of negotiation, would likely have asked for territory in exchange for its consent. In other words, it would have negotiated partition.

Partitionists respect and rely upon the power of the Canadian constitution. Before 17 April 1982, the federal government could create new provinces and accept additional territory into the Canadian federation, as it did in 1949 when Newfoundland became the tenth province. Since 1982, a general amending formula has been necessary to create new provinces. The governor-general, with the authorization of the houses of the federal Parliament, can also enact amendments that would change the borders of a given province — provided that the province's assembly agrees to the change. If Quebec were to repudiate the constitution, as it would if it opted to make a unilateral declaration of independence, the federal authorities would be entitled to retain whatever parts of Quebec they thought fit, producing a de facto partition. The province will not, of course, lose any of its territory as long as it remains a province of Canada, and partitionists will have no need to resort to plan B.

Of deep concern to partitionists is the fact that Quebec currently lacks the constitutional processes and guarantees needed to prevent amendments to its "provincial constitution" without sufficiently large majorities. The Quebec government is asking the electorate for a blank cheque when it asks for a mandate to separate from Canada: it is requesting permission to invent its own rule of law as it goes along. This, alone, is a strong moral argument for staying in Canada.

Democratic Expression

Another issue encompassed by the partition movement is that of democratic expression. It is also one of
the most contentious issues of the separatist agenda.
Should a simple democratic majority vote be considered adequate justification for redefining an entire
country? Separatists have claimed that a fifty-percent-
plus-one vote, within Quebec, is a legitimate indica-
tion of majority opinion. To win a referendum by a
single vote is all they would require to embark on their
desired course of action.

This contention raises two types of question. The
first involves jurisdiction: What constitutes a legitimate
voting issue? When does the subject of a vote violate
the rights of those affected by its outcome? Some
decisions cannot be made by certain groups. As Stephen Scott asks: "Are four people in a lifeboat entitled
to vote 'democratically' to eat the fifth? Is Kamloops,
or Kapuskasing, or Cap-de-la-Madeleine entitled to
impose communism or capital punishment or cinema
censorship?"[1]

The second type of question is related to the fifty-
percent-plus-one figure. Is it appropriate? Separatists
have long said that it is, claiming that it may be
unequivocally accepted as the basis for intelligent
democracy. The authors of the recent C.D. Howe
report on secession, Patrick Monahan and Michael

---

[1] Stephen A. Scott, "Bordering on a Nightmare," *Gazette* 16 Oct.
1995: B3.

Bryant, propose a two-referendum model for a province attempting to separate from the federation, and agree that, based on international and Canadian precedents, a simple majority vote is sufficient. But while these precedents could perhaps apply to the first referendum (which is intended to initiate the negotiation process), there are few international and no Canadian precedents that could be applied to the second, decisive referendum.

I believe most people feel that the majority requirement and the extent of the vote (provincial or Canadawide) should be determined in light of the importance of the vote. Apparently, Jean-Pierre Derriennic was endorsing this approach when he wrote that article 356 of the Quebec civil code stipulates a two-thirds majority is necessary to dissolve a professional association: "This detail places the separatist leaders in a paradoxical situation: they must explain to us why, when disbanding a fishing club, certain precautions must be taken against the risk of an abuse of power by the majority, yet such precautions become useless when it comes to dividing a state."[1]

Furthermore, if separatists truly believe that the fifty-percent-plus-one figure is the absolute indicator of a democratic majority, then why do they insist that the Canadian constitution is invalid on the grounds that Quebec rejected it? As I have mentioned, ninety

---

1 Jean-Pierre Derriennic, *Nationalisme et démocratie: Réflexion sur les illusions des indépendantistes québécois* (Montreal: Boréal, 1995) 87. Author's translation.

percent of Canada's provinces signed it. The Supreme Court of Canada has upheld it as legally valid and binding, yet the constitution remains unacceptable to the self-proclaimed democrats of the Quebec nationalist movement.

Advocates of partition argue that the fifty-percent-plus-one figure is insufficient in a vote on separation. No group, they maintain, has the right to break up the country based on a so-called democratic simple-majority vote held within a province or other political subdivision. To do so would be to violate the constitution. Why reject majority rule? Because the fundamental question must be this: Does a particular group of people have the legal or moral right to resolve a question that affects many others? Would *any* group have the right to break up the sovereign country of Canada (or even, hypothetically, the independent state of Quebec) based on a referendum? Under the Canadian constitution and international law, every part of Canada belongs to all of its people. The people of Canada as a whole are entitled to say "yes" or "no" to Quebec independence, and if "yes," to impose whatever terms and conditions they please.

The government of Quebec is violating its professed belief in the principle of democratic expression by insisting on holding referendum after referendum until the separatist option is victorious. The referendum, ideally a useful tool for determining citizens' response to a question, is being exploited as a means of justifying a decision on secession that the Parti Québécois government has already made.

Effective Control

Yet another issue bearing on partition is that of effective control. Effective control is, essentially, the unique capability of a given state to create its own laws, administer them, tax its citizens, and so on. No group or individual has the right to wrest effective control from the state. Effective control is necessary to statehood. Within the world community at large, if doubt exists as to whether effective control has been achieved by a breakaway state, official recognition of that new state's existence will be delayed; established states are reluctant to interfere in civil conflicts and thus to risk antagonizing the embattled parent state.

Ultimately, effective control comes down to the question of force: Who could control a specific area? Achieving effective control does not necessarily mean resorting to military or terrorist actions: legal and social actions may be deployed instead, and often are. As Derriennic and others have warned, however, Canadians should not be lulled into a false sense of security by reflecting upon a national history relatively unmarred by outbreaks of violence.[1] (Canadians do have a strong tradition of being restrained in their violent responses to domestic troubles.)

In international legal circles, possession counts for ninety-nine one-hundredths of the law. The government of Quebec has announced that following its

---

1 See Jean-Pierre Derriennic, *Nationalisme* 112–13. Author's translation.

declaration of independence, it would assume complete responsibility for the administration of the province's legal and tax systems, as well as for international treaties.[1] Such an attempt to gain effective control without a formally negotiated agreement would put the Quebec and Canadian governments into serious legal — and possibly military — conflict. If, however, Quebec did manage to seize effective control from Canada successfully and conclusively, then, in accordance with that aspect of international law which addresses the primacy of possession, the international community could surmise that Quebec had fulfilled a basic requirement of statehood.

During the campaign leading up to the 1995 referendum, Jean-Marc Jacob of the Bloc Québécois, assuming the inevitability of a "yes" vote, sent a letter on official Bloc letterhead to Quebecers serving in the Canadian military inviting them to shift their allegiance to the soon-to-be-formed Quebec armed forces. The motive was precisely this: to ensure that the government of Quebec had the resources to maintain effective control of the province.

Effective control becomes an even more delicate issue when applied to dissident elements of a population. During the October Crisis of 1970, the federal government sent troops into the province at the request of Liberal premier Robert Bourassa. It did so under the War Measures Act with the aim of coun-

---

1 National Executive Council of the Parti Québécois, *Quebec in a New World*, trans. Robert Chodos (Toronto: Lorimer, 1994) 43.

tering the terrorist actions of the Front de Libération du Québec (FLQ). In this instance, the government of Canada took decisive action to retain effective control of its territory. Today, the government of Quebec is also implicated in this problematic issue. After it has made its UDI, how will it deal with those of its residents who argue that such a declaration is illegal and that they will obey only those laws, federal and provincial, that are valid under the Canadian constitution? Federal Intergovernmental Affairs Minister Stéphane Dion has explicitly stated that Canada would not use force against an independent Quebec; he and federal Native Affairs Minister Ron Irwin have asked Premier Bouchard to promise that his government, in turn, will not take violent measures to prevent the partition of Quebec after separation.[1] Bouchard has offered no such assurances.

Many partitionists have said they would resort to civil disobedience if it appeared to be the only means of assisting the Canadian government to retain effective control. If these partitionists can mount a well-organized pressure campaign against a revolutionary Quebec government — if a significant number of people refuse to pay taxes to such a government, or recognize its legal authority in any way — then it may become apparent to Quebec nationalists that the idea that the province can secede with its borders intact is

---

1 See Paul Wells, "Let's Rule Out Use of Force: Dion," *Gazette* 10 Feb. 1996: A1; Paul Wells, "Bouchard Can't Duck Violence Issue, Irwin Says," *Gazette* 14 Feb. 1996: A9.

an impractical one. An independent Quebec would face a serious test in the court of international opinion with regard to its treatment of these peaceful resisters. By carrying on with their lives in Quebec during the troubled time following a UDI, all the while claiming that only the federal government in Ottawa could speak for them and protect their interests, these partitionists would lend credence to the notion that Canada still retained true effective control over the breakaway territory.

Several commentators illuminate the strategic importance of the principle of effective control. Gordon Robertson points out that even though a UDI would clearly be illegal, if made, uncertainty and disruption would follow in its wake. Adherence to the rule of law, he asserts, would be the best way to ensure effective control under these circumstances. He reminds us that after a "yes" vote, some people might think that the rest of Canada would have a government that had "lost its moral authority," and would therefore have no legitimate spokesperson who could negotiate with Quebec. Since the period following a "yes" vote would not be the time to reestablish such representation, contingency legislation, subject to proclamation after a "yes" vote, should be debated and passed without further delay.[1] Monahan and Bryant state, "The key assumption underlying our analysis is that it is

---

[1] Gordon Robertson, "Contingency Legislation for a Quebec Referendum," Confederation 2000 Conference, Ottawa, 26 Feb. 1996.

imperative that Canada attempt to set down the ground rules governing secession of a province well in advance of the next referendum."[1] Again, the goal is to forestall anarchy by asserting effective control.

In their 1995 report *Sovereign Injustice: Forcible Inclusion of the James Bay Crees and Cree Territory into a Sovereign Quebec*, the Grand Council of the Crees list the nonviolent steps that the Canadian government could take to ensure that Canadian laws are still applied to Aboriginals in Quebec, regardless of the statements or actions of the province's secessionist government. Some of these steps would also help to maintain partition as a viable option for other federalist Quebecers.

The first would be,

i) Court challenges in Canadian courts to emphasize the unconstitutionality, illegality, and illegitimacy of the PQ government's unilateral declaration of independence, accompanying legislation, and ensuing acts.

Such challenges would be necessary to signal in the strongest possible terms the Canadian government's rejection of all actions and declarations of a revolutionary Quebec government. The federal government's decision to refer the UDI issue to the Supreme Court

---

1 Patrick J. Monahan and Michael J. Bryant with Nancy C. Côté, *Coming to Terms with Plan B: Ten Principles Governing Secession,* Secession Papers, *C.D. Howe Institute Commentary* June 1996: 3.

is an example. However, unless all challenges are resolved *before* a referendum is called or a UDI is made, events will unfold too quickly for legal rulings to have any effect. While the Quebec government has stated that it does not believe the Canadian courts have the jurisdiction to stop the democratic will of the Quebec people, and while the ultimate answer to the Quebec question will probably not be a legal one, legal action must still be taken: the alternative is to forfeit the rule of law as well as effective control. The subsequent steps are as follows:

ii) Issuance of a declaration that Quebec remains a part of Canada, thereby discouraging or denying international recognition of a secessionist Quebec by third party states;

iii) Continued recognition of legitimate representatives of the Quebec population, including members of the House of Commons and Senate, under *Canada's Parliament of Canada Act*;

iv) Continued recognition of Aboriginal peoples in Quebec as nationals and citizens of their own respective nations and of Canada (if they so desire);

v) Continued (if not increased) application of federal, as well as Aboriginal laws, in at least some regions of the province of Quebec;

vi) Collection of income and other taxes from the Quebec population;

vii) Maintenance of Canadian airports and seaports, as well as customs and border officials at us-Canada border crossings in Quebec;

viii) Provision of federal programs and services to Aboriginal peoples, in accordance with the desires of the peoples concerned, their treaty rights and Canadian law;

ix) Provision of additional programs and services to Aboriginal peoples in Quebec in those territories where Aboriginal peoples refuse to recognize the claimed jurisdiction of a seceding Quebec, in order to make up for any loss of programs and services from Quebec;

x) Discussions with major third party states, with a view to ensuring that no international recognition is given to a secessionist Quebec state;

xi) Renegotiation of existing treaties with Aboriginal peoples in northern Quebec, including boundary questions. This would be necessary in light of an attempt by a secessionist Quebec to unilaterally assume all treaty obligations of the Canadian government contrary to the spirit and letter of these treaties.[1]

These steps were designed as tools to demonstrate to the world that Quebec will remain part of Canada until a legal separation can be negotiated. Ideally,

---

1 Grand Council of the Crees, *Sovereign Injustice* 166–68.

such measures would help persuade a secessionist government to abandon its threat to declare independence unilaterally and to adopt a legal means of acquiring effective control. Ottawa's delinquency in formulating its own measures to counter the Quebec government's drive towards secession very nearly proved catastrophic: hours before the result of the 1995 referendum was determined, Jacques Parizeau taped a victory speech for broadcast, indicating just how rapidly his government was prepared to establish independence.[1]

Self-Determination

The issue of whether Quebecers are a people in their own right is also related to the partition movement. And if they can be defined as a people, are they recognized as such under international law for the purposes of self-determination? Quebec nationalists insist that they do merit this recognition, seeing it as a vital element of their independence plan. Ironically, the five international experts whom the Quebec National Assembly commissioned in 1992 to study the effects of sovereignty maintained that Quebecers cannot claim the right to self-determination on the grounds that they are a subjugated people, and generally

---

1 See Sarah Scott, "Parizeau's Victory Speech Made It Clear There Was No Turning Back," *Gazette* 20 Feb. 1996: A3, B3.

provided little support for the PQ government's quest for people status.[1]

The United Nations has never officially defined what it means by "a people" — the definition literally depends on the current politics of its general assembly. It is clear, however, that a people embodies a series of traits that are both objective and subjective. Objectively, a people can be comprised of those who share a language, culture, tradition, and/or history. Subjectively — and far more importantly — a people is made up of individuals who demonstrate a common determination to live together and be considered as a unit, as well as an awareness of being a people.[2] Can the residents of Quebec claim to be a people on the basis of either of these sets of traits — objective or subjective? Quebec society has become increasingly cosmopolitan; the objective definition is, of course, untenable. On referendum night in October 1995, a majority of Quebec voters rejected the Parti Québécois government's vision of Quebec as an independent state. So, for nationalists to claim that Quebecers conform to the subjective definition of a people is clearly absurd.

---

1 See T. Franck, R. Higgins, A. Pellet, M. Shaw, and C. Tomuschat, "L'intégrité territoriale du Québec dans l'hypothèse de l'accession à la souveraineté," *Les attributs d'un Québec souverain*, Commission d'études des questions afférentes à l'accession du Québec à la souveraineté, Exposés et études 1 (Quebec: Bibliothèque nationale du Québec, 1992).

2 For the idea that the definition of a "people" has objective and subjective aspects, I am indebted to Brent Tyler, remarks, Special Committee on Canadian Unity Debate, Montreal, 16 Feb. 1996.

Another important element of the nationalist claim that Quebecers are a people, however, is unique to the Quebec-Canada situation and therefore transcends any international definitions, precedents, or rules: the two-nations theory. Its proponents state that Canada is the result of a pact forged in 1867 between two founding nations, the English and the French. Quebec nationalists, most of whom support this theory, use it to justify separation by maintaining that as a distinct founding nation of Canada, Quebecers are a distinct people; as such they have an internationally recognized right to self-determination, which they believe they can extend to encompass a right to secession.

Such justification is ultimately false, because today Quebec's boundaries delineate an administrative region, not a people. The current population of Quebec could only be defined as a people if that definition was stretched to the point that it could apply to almost *any* group. Nationalists often attempt to cloud this issue. Stephen Scott observes that while he was premier, Jacques Parizeau would argue, "the (francophone) Québécois majority are a *people*," and then "shif[t] his ground to insist that *Quebec as a province* has a right to independence as *one indivisible unit*."[1]

In his recent book *La partition du Québec: De Lord Durham à Stéphane Dion*, Claude Charon — an ardent antipartitionist who believes English Canada has been

1 Stephen A. Scott, "Issues Relating to Quebec Independence," public meeting address, Montreal, 19 Feb. 1992.

trying to dismember Quebec since its inception — also misrepresents the province's social makeup in his zeal to build a compelling case for independence. Quebec, he insists, is a poor, beleaguered French nation that must continually resist English Canada's attempts to crush it out of existence. Charon maintains that Quebec nationalism "is concerned with proving that the feeble autonomy that French Canadians managed to wrest from England and the anglophone elites in 1867 has, in spite of a centralizing federation, permitted the creation of a modern society in Quebec."[1] No mention is made of the vital historical role played by English-speaking Quebecers in creating the modern society; no consideration is given to French Canadians who have made lives for themselves in other parts of Canada; no recognition is granted to the many peoples of different ethnic backgrounds whose contribution to the province's development is incalculable. Evidently, Charon's vision excludes Aboriginal peoples as well. Charon's is a nationhood based solely on language.

Yet these simple facts are undeniable. French Canadians live throughout the country. (A large proportion of Acadians and other French-speaking Canadians are not in favour of Quebec separation.[2] They feel

1 Claude Charon, *La partition du Québec: De Lord Durham à Stéphane Dion* (Montreal: VLB, 1996) 61. Author's translation.

2 See Linda Cardinal and J-Yvon Thériault, "La francophonie canadienne et acadienne confrontée au défi québécois," *Répliques aux détracteurs de la souveraineté du Québec*, ed. Alain-G. Gagnon and François Rocher (Montreal: VLB, 1992) 329–41.

as though they have been written off by those with whom they share the traits of a people. The Fédération des francophones hors Québec has changed its name to Fédérations des communautés francophone et acadienne du Canada.) A number of English Canadians live inside the province of Quebec. There are now many people whose ancestry is neither French nor English living in Quebec. (It would be unfair to ask them to choose sides identified by pre-Confederation labels; they or their forebears chose to emigrate to Canada, not to English or French Canada.)

Aboriginals, of course, categorically reject the two-founding-nations idea — it amounts to a denial of their very existence. They, in fact, have by far the strongest claim to people status. Ironically, the Canadian government's restrictive policy of withdrawing the native rights of those Aboriginals who elect to live away from the reserves has served to strengthen that claim. Each Aboriginal group has a name. Each has a distinct language, history, culture, and tradition. Collectively, Aboriginals have a desire to live together as a people and a keen awareness of their status as a people.

Their collective vision was manifested just prior to the 1995 Quebec referendum when three Native groups held their own votes on sovereignty. The Crees of northern Quebec were over ninety-six percent in favour of remaining part of Canada, regardless of the outcome of the Quebec referendum; the Inuit rejected the idea of a sovereign Quebec by a vote of over ninety-five percent; and the Innu (Montagnais) did the same with a vote of ninety-nine percent. These groups had a voter turnout of just over seventy-five percent; many voters were out on the land and had to make special trips to the polling stations. In light of this, the idea that the fifty-percent-plus-one formula is an adequate tool for gauging consensus seems even more far-fetched.

The Quebec National Assembly recognized Aboriginals as distinct peoples in 1985. Aboriginal groups have taken on (to varying degrees, depending upon their individual circumstances) some of the tasks of self-government.[1] Some Aboriginal groups inhabit ancestral lands that span two or more provinces and/or territories. This is a result of perplexing European map-making practices, but it does lend substance to the argument that Aboriginal peoples living outside of a given province or territory should have a say, on behalf of those of their people who reside within it, in what happens there, if only on moral grounds.

Ultimately, it is only Aboriginals who can honestly exploit the notion of being a people to achieve their political ends. While Quebec nationalists contort themselves in their efforts to define Quebecers as a people with the right to self-determination, Aboriginals have no need to defend their status as they struggle to remain Canadian. If the separatists succeed, Aboriginal peoples may then proceed to implement the partition of the independent state of Quebec with-

---

1 The Crees maintain an office in Ottawa, which is called the Embassy of the Cree Nation.

out becoming entangled in the kind of legal and moral web that will surely ensnare others.

Setting the issue of people status aside, we are still faced with the question of who has the inherent right to self-determination. Quebecers already enjoy this right; they have a great deal of political freedom and opportunity, they play a crucial role in the formation of both Canadian and Quebec societies, and they have access to economic opportunity. Despite decades, even centuries, of anxiety that it would be lost, Quebec has retained the French language and with it a sense of cultural identity. The government of Quebec has lobbied for and been granted by the federal government powers in the areas of taxation, immigration, and manpower training. Ottawa has proven itself to be flexible in its efforts to accommodate the special interests of the residents of the province.

The government of Quebec has not demonstrated a similar desire for accommodation when it comes to dealing with the groups over which it has jurisdiction. Partitionists and others who insist that Quebec nationalists cannot claim the right to self-determination and then deny it to other groups are wilfully misunderstood or ignored by the Parti Québécois government. Aboriginals have historically had their right to self-determination infringed upon; their land has been transferred between governments without their input, consent, or even knowledge. Still, the Quebec government feels justified in continuing this practice, maintaining that Aboriginal peoples' right to self-determination, their "right of autonomy within

Quebec," is limited by provincial law.[1] Separatists assert that the province's present boundaries are sacred; they are inviolate, even in the event of a UDI. The hypocrisy here is monumental and must be strenuously resisted.

Secessionist self-determination is, naturally, an entirely different matter. The UN, upholder of the right to self-determination of peoples, does not generally recognize it. International-law experts see self-determination and secession as "two distinct and separate concepts," and maintain that the UN Charter recognizes a right to self-determination only "in limited circumstances": "More specifically, self-determination, including a right to secede, was to be expressly recognized for those colonized peoples in the Non-Self-Governing Territories and Trust Territories referred to in the Charter."[2] Quebec, obviously, cannot be included in this category. Scott adds: *"Canada as a whole, and in all its parts, belongs to all of its people, so far as sovereignty is concerned."* Furthermore, "A colonial right of self-determination can have no relevance to the population of Quebec, which is not governed by others."[3]

A key element of UN policy is the principle that a state has the right to exist without being subjected to threats from external or internal sources. With the aim

---

1 Eric Gourdeau, "La souveraineté: Une chance unique pour les autochrones d'acquérir leur pleine autonomie," Gagnon and Rocher, eds., *Répliques* 86–87. Author's translation.

2 Grand Council of the Crees, *Sovereign Injustice* 55, 37–38.

3 Stephen A. Scott, "Issues."

of encouraging states to permit all sectors of their populations, especially minorities, the right to self-determination within the overarching structure of the state, the UN stipulates that these minorities only have the right to secede if they are former colonies that have not yet been given their political freedom. There has been some debate about allowing groups that have been seriously disenfranchised to secede as an extension of the laws enabling former colonies to secede. Quebec, however, is neither a former colony of Canada nor is it disenfranchised.

Neither would partitionists qualify as a disenfranchised group under international law. But again, if we look more closely at the partitionist position within the context of the separatist position, an interesting inversion takes place. Rather than attempting to secede from an independent Quebec, partitionists would actually be struggling to hold on to territory that would remain part of Canada: they would be fighting for the right to self-determination in order *not* to secede from Canada.[1]

Violence

Finally, the most volatile issue that relates to the partition movement is that of violence. Partitionists who, in attempting to assess the conditions that will affect their course of action, allude to the possibility that

---

1 See Patrick J. Monahan and Michael J. Bryant 35.

violent actions could erupt from the complex of political tensions that comprise Quebec society today are censured by fellow federalists and by Quebec nationalists alike. They stand accused of inciting such actions, of taking a negative position, simply by warning that these actions could occur and, of course, by announcing their intention of partitioning a seceding Quebec.

Here a familiar double standard is evoked. In 1991, Parizeau "declared that he would count on the Canadian army to ensure peace in the period following a declaration of independence." In 1994, Jacques Brassard (at that time the Parti Québécois whip) declared that the "forces of order" could be deployed to guarantee the territorial integrity of Quebec, identifying "Aboriginal peoples and other dissident groups" as targets.[1] Those, like Parizeau and Brassard, who announce their intention to partition Canada and threaten to back it up by using military force against dissenters generally escape censure. They are appeased or supported. Censure is reserved for partitionists.

Raymond Villeneuve, head of the Mouvement de la libération nationale du Québec, publishes a newsletter named *La tempête* that describes anglophones and allophones as enemies of Quebec. It even goes so far as to list the names and telephone numbers of business leaders the *mouvement* considers a threat to the province's sovereigntist aspirations. While the Quebec government has denounced the language and outlook of these people, it has not, to date, sought to restrain

---

1 Qtd. in Grand Council of the Crees, *Sovereign Injustice* 158–59.

its activities by means of human-rights and hate literature legislation. In December of 1995, the Anglophone Assault Group briefly entered into the national spotlight when it sent an unsigned letter to the media "threatening to assassinate Lucien Bouchard and to commit violence against Quebec separatists."[1] (The group has taken no action and has not been heard from since, leading many to believe the whole thing was a hoax.)

A society that can spawn such groups needs leaders committed to defusing the conditions that make them possible. A peaceful example must be set unambiguously and consistently. Matthew Coon Come has categorically rejected the use of organized violence on behalf of the Crees of Northern Quebec. Zebedee Nungak, president of the Makivik Society, which represents the province's Inuit population, has done the same. Premier Bouchard has yet to offer similar assurances.

1 Aaron Derfel, "Anglophone Leaders Decry Letter," *Gazette* 29 Dec. 1995: AI.

Implementing Partition: Some Strategies and Proposals

There are two basic strategies that the government of Quebec could use in its attempt to secede from Canada: it could pursue separation through legal means or make a unilateral declaration of independence. If it chooses the legal strategy, it must, of course, focus its energies on amending the constitution. It would have to request that a constitutional conference be called, after a secession deal had been worked out, at which all the provinces and the federal government could review the proposed changes.

This conference would be the culmination of a process whereby Quebec would have negotiated with Canada all the issues surrounding its departure, including the dividing of assets, the apportioning of debt, and the delimiting of the territory that would be removed from the country; the right to travel freely and customs and free-trade issues would also have to be hammered out. These issues are all contentious, but the two most divisive are the sharing of the national debt and the partitioning of Quebec, especially if

Canada demands large tracts of land such as the northern sector of the province or a territorial link with the rest of Canada.

The federal government is bound by its fiduciary responsibility to the Aboriginal peoples in the North and throughout Quebec; it must ensure territorial contiguity (either by negotiating a corridor through the newly independent state or by retaining a viable land transportation corridor between Ontario and New Brunswick); it must seriously consider that certain predominantly federalist parts of Quebec — for instance, the Pontiac region, the Eastern Townships, western Montreal, and the eastern north shore of the St. Lawrence River — could demand its support in their struggle for partition. All these concerns and commitments would play pivotal roles in talks leading to a legally negotiated separation.

The discussion would necessarily be involved and protracted and emotionally wearing for most Canadians. If the government of Quebec chose to embark on this legal path towards separation, it would not be able to deliver on its promise to be done with Canada, once and for all. But it would have demonstrated its respect for the democratic process. In this sad yet civilized scenario, separation would be legitimized by the constitution and partition would be legitimized by negotiations aimed at preserving Canada's viability and the fundamental rights of its citizens.

The second secession strategy — an illegal UDI — would likely be implemented this way: the Quebec government would simply state that, as of a specified date, the province would be independent, and that it would have the right to separate keeping all of its existing territory. The apparent simplicity of this statement masks a world of instability and confusion: a UDI would, in effect, be a coup-d'état. What laws would apply to Quebec residents after such a declaration? How would all the outstanding issues be resolved? How could peace be maintained in an environment of confusion and fear? How could partition be negotiated rationally? Partitionists wish to avoid this scenario at all costs, yet it almost became a reality with the 1995 referendum.

Map-Based Partition

There are essentially two ways of dividing up a territory: according to a simple map-based plan, by which each group involved lays claim to a specific territory, regardless of the wishes of that territory's inhabitants; or according to a vote-based plan, by which the majority within a certain unit (a poll, a municipality, a region, or a riding) chooses which state it will join. Some partition advocates (such as Monahan and Bryant) propose a mix of the two models: map-based for Aboriginal peoples and vote-based for other communities. Among the grass-roots organizations that advocate partition, however, consensus on the boundaries that should be accepted by Canada as the price for letting Quebec secede is elusive. This question of borders is one of the hardest for partitionists to answer.

Quebec nationalists were naturally among the first to ask them how they would divide Quebec territory in an equitable way and how they would implement partition. Who gets what? How are these decisions rationalized and justified? But while such questions are undeniably valid, the answers to them are necessarily complex. Though many separatists insist that partitionists have defensible answers immediately, they themselves have become masters at dodging similar questions, and at presenting patently unworkable or even illegal solutions to them. One prime example is Lucien Bouchard's comment about separation being "a magic wand" that will make all of Quebec's problems vanish.[1]

Some proponents of map-based partition — among the first were William Shaw and Lionel Albert, whose seminal 1980 book *Partition: The Price of Quebec's Independence* has drawn a great deal of nationalist fire — depend on historical arguments. A quick overview of Canada's territorial history may therefore prove useful in assessing these arguments. In 1670, King Charles of England gave the land that drained into Hudson Bay to the Hudson's Bay Company. He did so without considering the rights of the Aboriginals who inhabited the area, and thereby initiated the series of wrongs that is the justification for current First Nations claims to the right of self-determination.

Named Rupert's Land, the new territory comprised

1 See "Bouchard's Magic and White Babies," editorial, *Gazette* 17 Oct. 1995: B2.

much of the northern part of what would later become Canada (see map 1, p. 58) — specifically, portions of Quebec, Ontario, Manitoba, the Northwest Territories, and Nunavut (the new Inuit territory that will soon be created from the eastern section of the Northwest Territories). New France never had a claim upon this territory, and so Quebec does not have a historical claim to it now, despite the poetic preamble to the Parti Québécois' Bill 1 (published just prior to the referendum), which says that "the heart of this land [Quebec] beats in French."[1]

In 1867, Canada came into being. In 1870, the Rupert's Land and North-Western Territory Order granted Rupert's Land to Canada; specifically, it was given to the federal government to administer. Then, in 1898, some of Rupert's Land was transferred to the provinces. This transfer was undertaken with the implicit understanding that Quebec was, and would remain forever, a province of Canada. The Quebec Boundaries Extension Act of 1912 transferred the remaining part of the peninsula north of the 1898 border to Quebec. The official name of that territory was changed from Ungava to New Quebec.

In 1927, Britain's Privy Council ruled that all lands in what was then northern Quebec whose waters drain into the Atlantic Ocean were to belong to Newfoundland, then a British colony. This newly created territory was called Labrador. Quebec has never recognized the

---

1 *Projet de loi sur l'avenir du Québec* (Quebec: Gouvernement du Québec, 1995) 8. Official translation.

Privy Council ruling.[1] The province's refusal to do so reveals a fundamental hypocrisy: add land, and we will acknowledge it immediately; remove land, and we will cling to our old borders.

Henri Brun, in his 1992 essay "L'intégrité territoriale d'un Québec souverain," examines the question of whether Quebec would lose a significant portion of its territory if it were to make a UDI. Speaking from a nationalist perspective, he admits that although Quebec must follow the constitution while it is a Canadian province, after a UDI it would be bound only by international law. The principles of *uti possidetis* and effective control, which stipulate that seceding states can keep the territories they possess at the time of secession if they are able to demonstrate their ability to fulfil consistently all the responsibilities that belong to a state, would then come into effect.[2] Brun, incredibly, seems to be arguing that Quebec may choose the particular set of laws by which it will be bound on the basis of convenience. He is silent as to how Quebec will become sovereign without committing an illegal act or losing territory to Canada during the negotiations required to forge constitutional amendments.

While Brun explores territorial issues from a Quebec-nationalist vantage point, Shaw and Albert redraw the map from a federalist position. In *Partition: The*

---

1 This territorial history has been paraphrased from Grand Council of the Crees, *Sovereign Injustice* 199–202.

2 Henri Brun, "L'intégrité territoriale d'un Québec souverain," Gagnon and Rocher, eds., *Répliques* 70.

Price of Quebec's Independence, they present a historical case for Canada's right to keep the northern Quebec territories, the south shore of the St. Lawrence, the easternmost tip of the north shore of the St. Lawrence, the western half of the Island of Montreal (up to rue St-Denis), and the Outaouais in the event of Quebec's separation. The idea of losing this massive amount of territory would, ideally, serve as a powerful deterrent to the separatist project. The book is an attempt to dispel the "myths of entitlement" that were circulating among Quebec nationalists at the time and that have proven extremely persistent. The points Shaw and Albert make are still relevant.

They use historical documentation of land ownership to support their partition plan, and make this succinct statement in their introduction:

The present map of Canada, with its provincial boundaries, is a product of the division of powers within the British colonial administration since 1763 as they have evolved through Confederation. The people and Parliament of Canada enjoy sovereignty over the land mass of Canada, and only the people, acting through Parliament, can add (as it has) to Quebec's territory, or agree (as it might) to just what part of Quebec's territory it might give up to a foreign country; for a sovereign French country would be a foreign country.[1]

---

1   Shaw and Albert, *Partition* 18.

Another approach to the question of map-based partition would be to consider which regions of the province have demonstrated their support for the principles of federalism. A map highlighting these regions would present a pattern of resistance to illegal separation from Canada: it would present a graphic proposal for partition. As I have mentioned, the Aboriginal inhabitants of Quebec's northern land (the Cree, the Inuit, and the Innu) have shown that they wish to remain part of Quebec by organizing their own referendums that yielded massive "no" majorities. The easternmost section of the Gaspé Peninsula, the north shore of the St. Lawrence River directly below Labrador, and certain sections of the Eastern Townships are predominantly English-speaking areas and have historically been bastions of federalism, as has the Pontiac-Outaouais region of the province. Montreal — specifically its western sectors — is heavily federalist as well. Encompassing sixty percent of the provincial tax base, the densely populated city would be a vital element of the newly partitioned province or the independent state of Quebec, so it is here that the toughest partition battles would be fought.

Partitionists engaged in remapping a postsecession Quebec — most notably the members of William Shaw's new group, the Preparatory Committee for the Partition of Quebec — often take into account the fact that Canada would need a land corridor through the province linking Ontario and Atlantic Canada. This would serve as a lifeline, ensuring that the country as constituted by the remaining provinces would remain

Map-Based Partition

RUPERT'S LAND

Land added to Quebec in 1898 and 1912

A CANADIAN CORRIDOR

East-west connecting corridor containing
the St. Lawrence Seaway, Trans-Canada
Highway, and Canadian National Railway

FEDERALIST QUEBEC

Traditionally federalist regions

THE FINAL RESULT

Source: The Preparatory Committee for the Partition of Quebec

MAP 1

58

viable. The current Quebec government's assurances that Canadian goods and people could pass freely through the new state of Quebec ring hollow for many. If our ally to the south could pass legislation such as the Helms-Burton Bill, then what would prevent Quebec from attempting to influence Canadian policymaking through border controls? Such controls would be a powerful tool for pressuring Canada to accept Quebec's demands during postsecession negotiations.

If Canada retained the northern portion of Quebec, it would have a land link via Labrador, but this would not be adequate: the detour is simply too long to be economically feasible, and it is impossible to build permanent roads and rail links using current construction technology on ground that is frozen much of the year. Also, from a purely psychological viewpoint, Canadians have a blind spot when it comes to the North: they consider it remote, inaccessible — an unlikely choice as a crucial land bridge.

Inevitably, partitionists will find their attention drawn to the south shore of the St. Lawrence River. Most of the St. Lawrence Seaway's infrastructure is located on the south shore, as are the land links that connect Ontario to the Atlantic provinces. Also, since Canada would want a slice of the St. Lawrence River for itself, it is not difficult to foresee that the federal government would endeavour to retain all of the south shore.

All these map-based partition arguments would, of course, be aggressively resisted by Quebec nationalists. The northern territories are home to one of the massive hydroelectric dams — at James Bay — that the Quebec government has built over the years; hydro-electricity is among the most powerful of Quebec's economic resources. Hydro-Québec, the province's own utility, has an emotional significance for many Quebecers: the rallying cry of the movement to nation-alize the industry was "maître chez nous." Although it would cause Quebecers great economic pain and emo-tional distress to lose the James Bay hydroelectric project, those who buy into the separatist argument would surely have to face the fact that the right to self-determination they claim for themselves must also be extended to the Aboriginal inhabitants of the northern regions who fervently wish to remain part of Canada, and who have traditionally made their home in what is now Quebec for a much longer time than any other residents of the province.

The dilemma for Quebec nationalists confronting this situation becomes clear: choose the moral high ground and accept the loss of these territories, or choose to be duplicitous and use narrow and specious legalistic arguments (as does Brun) to deny Abori-ginals the right to self-determination. The Quebec government could also try to seize effective control and fight for the territory, or negotiate some sort of compromise: a revenue/cost-sharing arrangement be-tween Quebec and the Aboriginal groups involved, and a joint-venture corporation to administer the dams.

If Canadians feel threatened by the prospect of having to go through a foreign country to get to the other portion of their own country, Quebecers will feel the same way if they have to travel through the Canadian south shore of the St. Lawrence to get to the United States. Negotiated corridors have been proposed as a solution, but they present an array of new problems. Ultimately, no one can predict exactly what effect the initiatives of partitionists will have on the map of an independent Quebec. More debate on the issue should be initiated now; further exploration and an ongoing evaluation of fresh ideas are required.

Vote-Based Partition

Having looked closely at these multifaceted options for the map-based division of an independent Quebec, partitionists will have to examine the equally complex possibility of vote-based partition. Some see it as a more equitable way of dividing up territory. A number of different approaches to this form of partition were discussed in the national media early in 1996 when Prime Minister Jean Chrétien appointed Quebecers Stéphane Dion and Pierre Pettigrew to his cabinet and the issue was raised publicly by the governmental establishment for the first time.

Right after the 30 October 1995 referendum, some members of the partition movement suggested that the provincial ridings that voted against secession should stay in Canada, either as separate provinces or as annexes to Ontario, New Brunswick, or the new

Vote-Based Partition (by Riding)

Quebec

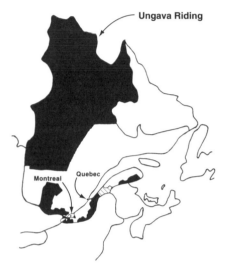

Ungava Riding

Montreal   Quebec

Quebec City Region

Montreal Region

■ = Partition based upon the 1995 referendum results

▨ = Further partition based on the CROP prediction that "yes" votes would
    drop by 3% if voters were told some partitioning was inevitable

Map Source: Commission de la représentation électorale du Québec, 1992
Results Source: Directeur général des élections du Québec, 1995

MAP 2

territory of Nunavut. Others pointed out the complications inherent in this formula, and called for a consideration of such factors as past referendum results, the ethnicity of a given riding's population, and the nature of its representation in Parliament (Bloc Québécois or Liberal).

Riding-based partition is possible, since by law ridings must be viable regions. Even though riding configuration has changed frequently over the years, and will change again in 1997, the viability requirement provides some stability. It is significant that all of the ridings that voted "no" in the 1995 referendum either share a boundary line with Canada or the United States, or border on the St. Lawrence River; so if the secessionists had taken the vote and the partitionists had subsequently prevailed, there would have been no untenable, Quebec-surrounded enclaves.

Map 2 illustrates the effects of partitioning based on the results of the 1995 referendum, showing ridings with a federalist majority in black. To determine how a partition mandate could effect the vote, the CROP poll on partition taken after the 1995 referendum will be used to adjust the figures. This map demonstrates what happens when the "yes" vote is reduced by three percent: the additional ridings that would have had a federalist majority are shaded. And it is possible than in an actual partition vote, the secessionist vote reduction would be even greater.

Another approach to vote-based partition is to ask municipalities and rural regions directly where their allegiance lies; this has been suggested by Dion and by Monahan and Bryant. Such a tactic could, however, result in a patchwork-quilt effect: if several of these units opted to remain Canadian, they could find themselves reborn as isolated enclaves within an independent Quebec, cut off from the borders or the waterways that would guarantee them access to Canada. It would also shift an extremely divisive debate to the community level, subjecting the social fabric to a high degree of stress.

In his 1992 book *Canada Remapped: How the Partition of Quebec Will Reshape the Nation*, Scott Reid proposes that a referendum-based model be used to determine how an independent Quebec would be partitioned. Reid is highly critical of map-based partition strategies, insisting that they have been the root cause of most of the violence that has occurred during earlier partition struggles in other countries.

Claiming that in the past partition has failed for a consistent, identifiable set of reasons, Reid suggests these precautions: "Partition must take place before separation occurs," since "To attempt partition after . . . means that a single legal system can no longer be used to govern the land transfer process"; if this were to occur, then the only course of action would be to use force, and this is to be avoided at all costs. "Partition must be democratic. The desires of the inhabitants of any given area must have priority over all other considerations . . . ." Finally, "The separatists must be involved in the partition process. Involvement encourages participation and disarms attempts to stalemate or boycott the democratic partition process."[1]

Reid later adds — after a discussion in which he describes the partitioning of the Swiss canton of Berne as "a model for Canada" — that voting on partition should be conducted "at the most local level possible" ("The smaller the voting units . . . the more people can become enfranchised in the country to which they feel they belong"), and that the "focus might be on self-determination only." This is because "historical, legal, and strategic concerns, or the ownership of fixed capital assets in the territory to be partitioned, aren't nearly as important [as self-determination] from a humane point of view."[2]

It is with statements such as this that Reid, driven by an admirable desire to veto any partition plan that would promote hostility between the two opposing sides, compounds an error. The poll-based (as opposed to municipality- or riding-based) partition vote that Reid advocates as the best means of enfranchising the largest possible number of individuals could only lead to a postsecession Quebec mottled with thousands of tiny federalist enclaves — approximately sixty thousand by Reid's own count.[3] His solution is to declare that enclaves close to, bordering on, or connected (in certain instances by some kind of sovereign corridor) to Canada or the ocean or the

---

1 Scott Reid, *Canada Remapped: How the Partition of Quebec Will Reshape the Nation* (Vancouver: Pulp, 1992) 22.

2 Scott Reid, *Canada Remapped* 36.

3 Scott Reid, *Canada Remapped* 103–04.

United States could be maintained, but that all others would be too costly; it would also be too difficult to ensure that the transportation links serving them would always remain open. Unworkable enclaves would have to be turned over to the new state of Quebec.

Reid envisions that we would be left with four major enclaves in western Quebec and the Eastern Townships, eight enclaves in the Gaspé, and a few in the extreme eastern portion of the north shore of the Gulf of St. Lawrence. But how could such an implementation scheme be justified? The residents of those thousands of enclaves turned over to an independent Quebec would see their votes count for nothing. Reid's humane imperative would be reversed. The disenfranchised federalists inhabiting unworkable enclaves would experience firsthand that sense of betrayal Aboriginal peoples felt when their lands were traded between governments.

In attempting to present the Swiss Jura-Berne canton partition as a model for Canadian partitionists Reid also misses a fundamental point: the Swiss and Canadian situations cannot be compared for any practical purpose because neither the newly partitioned canton of Jura nor the remaining canton of Berne were to become independent of the Swiss federation. The Swiss federal government oversaw the process. (It would actually have been interesting to see how Switzerland, with its almost fanatical approach to its own internal security, would have handled a canton's bid to secede.) The Canadian equivalent of the Jura-Berne case would be the bisection of one Canadian province with the federal government overseeing the process.

Finally, Reid, like so many others, errs in assuming that only Quebec anglophones and allophones want to remain a part of the Canadian federation. Clearly, there are many francophones who would be interested in staying Canadian, and eagerly anticipate the possibility of a "new deal with Canada." Overall, however, Reid does offer partitionists much food for thought as they endeavour to devise a feasible vote-based partition plan.

Two more problems that a purely vote-based partition system is likely to produce should be addressed here. The first is that this approach to partition does not guarantee territorial contiguity between Ontario and New Brunswick. As map 2 shows, if Quebec was redrawn according to how each of its ridings voted in a referendum on sovereignty, Canada would lose its contiguous southern land and sea links between Ontario and the Atlantic provinces. Worse still, the federalist Eastern Townships would be completely cut off, except for some access via the St. Lawrence River and the United States border. (Note: if Ungava riding were to vote for secession, then Canada would be cut into three pieces.)

This presents some grave concerns, and the idea of connecting these three areas with negotiated corridors is tenuous at best, especially given the heated atmosphere that would likely prevail after secession. Reid suggests that the Colón corridor, which connected the Panamanian city of Colón in the American-controlled

Canal Zone with the rest of Panama, could serve as a model.[1] This looks interesting, until one realizes that the Colón corridor was only ten kilometres long and that the world's most powerful nation was one of the two parties that signed the deal: Canadian corridors would be at least twenty and seventy kilometres long as the crow flies, and Canada does not have America's "big stick" policing authority.

Nor can Alaska be used as an example of a divided state's viability. Alaska is easily reached via international waters, whereas the St. Lawrence is a strategic bottleneck in the journey to and from Atlantic Canada; it could be plugged, under certain circumstances, with relative ease. The idea of access via the United States is not workable for the simple reason that it would leave Canada vulnerable to foreign political pressure: imagine the impact a Helms-Burton-type bill would have on the isolated Eastern Townships.

The second problem is that under a vote-based partition system the northern territories of Quebec — while encompassing the traditional lands of Aboriginal peoples who have clearly demonstrated their intention to remain part of Canada — could still be lost to the secessionists. The "no" side won the 1995 referendum by just twelve hundred votes; the results were split along racial lines, with the overwhelming majority of "yes" votes deriving from the non-Native sector of the local population. How difficult would it be for the Parti Québécois government (and/or Hydro-Québec)

---

1 Scott Reid, *Canada Remapped* 107–10.

to swing the next vote by assigning more civil servants (or employees) to the riding?

New Voices

The voices of Patrick Monahan and Michael Bryant are the most recent to join the debate on partition strategy. *Coming to Terms with Plan B: Ten Principles Governing Secession* appeared in June 1996, and the eighth principle it presents and explores is partition. The authors, who generally support the vote-based partition option, firmly refute the sovereigntist notion that Canadian constitutional law and international law would uphold Quebec's existing borders after the province achieved independence. Due to the absence of "any terms and conditions for secession" under the Canadian constitution and a similar lack of support in the realm of international law, "the territorial status quo remains unchanged; that is, the province remains a part of Canada" until it is released from the federation through negotiation and constitutional amendment.

Monahan and Bryant echo the unassailable truism that fuels the partition movement: "if Canada is divisible, then Quebec must also be divisible." They go on to point out in dramatically simple terms the profound hypocrisy at the heart of the nationalist drive for sovereignty; Quebec has committed itself to argue "that those voting for secession have a right not only to secede but also to require other identifiable groups to secede against their will. We know of no principled argument that would justify this result."[1]

Of the various arguments that have been mounted against the partition option, there is only one that Monahan and Bryant find difficult to reject out of hand: "there is no straightforward way to redraw [Quebec's] borders effectively without creating Canadian enclaves within Quebec that would be geographically isolated from the rest of Canada." It is in addressing this argument — whose proponents believe that partition is "totally impractical" — that Monahan and Bryant formulate their proposal for realizing partition. They claim that the complexities the enclave problem generates are not, as some would suggest, "insuperable," and evoke (as does Reid, of course) the Jura-Berne precedent as evidence (despite what I've described as its limited applicability to the Canadian situation).[2] Boiling down their observations, the authors distil a pair of "limiting principles": "Regions within Quebec that wished to remain within Canada would have to have a distinct legal status and an identifiable territory"; and "such regions would have to be territorially contiguous with Canada."

Monahan and Bryant conclude by remarking that although the task of dividing up a postsecession Quebec is fraught with difficulties, "it should be kept in mind that any impracticalities arising from partition

---

1 Patrick J. Monahan and Michael J. Bryant, *Coming to Terms* 35.

2 Patrick J. Monahan and Michael J. Bryant, *Coming to Terms* 36.

would hardly be the *cause* of federalists within Quebec but rather would represent another complicated *effect* of Quebec secession."[1]

---

1 Patrick J. Monahan and Michael J. Bryant, *Coming to Terms* 37.

Unique Circumstances: The Problem of Precedent

In attempting to present the secession of Quebec as a democratic and viable exercise, separatists often cite precedents. Partitionists, too, look to the example of other solutions to similar conflicts over territorial ownership in an effort to find a formula for preserving Canadian soil within an independent Quebec. The velvet divorce of Norway and Sweden is occasionally evoked by Quebec nationalists to prove that the province could separate painlessly from Canada using a unilateral declaration of independence; but there are many differences that prohibit easy comparisons.

In 1905, Norway's Parliament announced that the Swedish monarch was no longer the Norwegian monarch. With this announcement, Norway separated from Sweden, its borders intact. Norway has been a country since the tenth century. It is one of the oldest constitutional democracies in the world. When Napoleon's dominion finally collapsed in 1814 and he was forced to abdicate, Europe had to be remade. Denmark ceded Norway to Sweden, and though Norway retained its own military, monarchy, and constitution from 1814 to 1905, an absolute split was the goal it set for itself and eventually achieved with a minimum of complication and ill will. Sweden was in accord with Norway's wishes, but even if it had objected, it is doubtful that it could have prevailed over Norway in an armed struggle. If Quebec was to be comparable to Norway, it would have to have been an independent state at some point; it would require an already recognized constitution and a military force; it would need a fully functional state government.

Two other foreign examples are also put forward in such discussions: Western Australia's bid to secede from the Commonwealth in 1933–34 and Singapore's separation from Malaysia in 1965. The Western Australia example is one that Quebec nationalists would undoubtedly prefer to dismiss. A plebiscite was held on the issue of separation. Sixty-six percent voted in favour, and Western Australia requested an imperial amendment to the Australian constitution to make it possible. Britain, however, would not consider Western Australia's petition because it did not come from the government of Australia, which opposed separation.[1] The issue was thus put to rest.

In 1962, the electorate of Singapore voted in favour of joining Malaya and two other territories to form Malaysia. The federation came into existence in 1963. In 1965, Singapore separated from Malaysia after being federated for a mere two years.[2] The Republic

---

1 Grand Council of the Crees, *Sovereign Injustice* 333n1,168.

2 See Philippe Regnier, *Singapore: City-State in South-East Asia* (London: Hurst, 1991).

of Singapore has been upheld by some as a city-state model that could be applied to Montreal should it resolve to become independent of both a post-secessionist Quebec *and* Canada.

Partitionists sometimes draw a parallel between the two centres when envisioning Montreal as an eleventh province. It is doubtful, however, that Montreal could function as a city-state. Singapore has a terrifically advantageous geographical location — it was a booming port long before its Malaysia involvement. Montreal is also a strategically located port city, but it could hardly be described as booming these days; unlike Singapore, it is not (and will not be for the foreseeable future) in a position to offer the kind of generous tax incentives necessary to attract and maintain foreign investment. Singapore, in an effort to avoid economic collapse after the dissolution of the Malay federation, opened its doors to multinational companies and lured them in with such enticements as a low-cost work force; Montreal could not offer such bonuses for obvious reasons — its need to belong to NAFTA among them. With its weakened economy, Montreal would be unlikely to survive the transition to city-state.

There are two domestic precedents, as well, that serve to excite debate within the context of the current conflict. The first bears a strong resemblance to the example of Western Australia. "In 1868, Nova Scotia petitioned the Imperial Parliament for an amendment to enable the province to secede from Canada. At that time, nearly two-thirds of the voters had signed a petition in favour of secession. However the petition was denied since it did not emanate from the federal government in Canada."[1]

Quebec nationalists, of course, look instead to the case of Newfoundland. They attempt to justify their resolve to leave Canada based on a simple referendum majority by citing as precedent Newfoundland's decision to join Canada based on the same margin. Again, the justification is false. Prior to becoming Canada's tenth province, Newfoundland was a colony of Great Britain. Although it had been given responsible government in 1855, Newfoundland's economy was so badly decimated by the Great Depression that it had to relinquish the right to self-government to Britain in exchange for financial assistance. When World War II ended in 1945, Newfoundland had to decide whether to set its sights on regaining its independence, remain under British control, or join Canada. It chose the third course of action, and held two referendums in its quest to secure the support of its electorate.

Monahan and Bryant include a description in their report of how these referendums were set and explain their outcome. Voters were asked to choose one of three scenarios: "1) Commission of Government [controlled by Britain] for a period of five years; 2) Confederation with Canada; 3) Responsible government as it existed in 1933." The third "was the most favored choice, but it had drawn only about 45 percent of the vote. So the electorate returned to the polls . . . for a second referendum that dropped the first option,

---

1 Grand Council of the Crees, *Sovereign Injustice* 333n1,167.

which had received only 14 percent in the first referendum. Confederation won about 52 percent of the vote, enough to trigger the opening of negotiations."[1]

For several reasons, Newfoundland's joining Canada is not a viable precedent for Quebec's departure. Although the determination of the people of Newfoundland to seek union with Canada was revealed by their own plebiscite vote, it was the British Parliament's involvement that legitimized the process. The plebiscite only provided the moral go-ahead; it did not furnish Newfoundland with the legal right to initiate the procedure of joining the federation of Canadian provinces on its own behalf. In short, Britain and Canada were in agreement as to the annexation of Newfoundland; no such accord exists in the Quebec situation.

Another interesting point of comparison may be found in the Newfoundland case. The Parliament of Canada did not have to consult the other provinces in making its decision to admit Newfoundland as the tenth province. The Newfoundland plebiscite was a useful tool to ensure that the majority of the colony's voters were prepared to become Canadian; but within Canada, in 1949, the federal Parliament was empowered to act on behalf of its citizens without seeking a further mandate. While bound by the constitutional provision to consult with an affected province if its borders are to be changed, the government did not then need to seek a national consensus before it

---

1 Patrick J. Monahan and Michael J. Bryant, *Coming to Terms* 13.

annexed Newfoundland. It took Canada's consent for Newfoundland to join the Canadian federation; it would take Canada's consent for it to leave.

It is the lack of a separation clause in the constitution that would necessitate a constitutional conference leading to a constitutional amendment on the issue of Quebec secession. Newfoundland's case is the opposite of Quebec's. The territorial integrity of Canada was not jeopardized by its annexation of Newfoundland; it was actually strengthened. Also, if Newfoundland were to leave Canada today, it would not geographically split the country into two pieces, nor would it block a large portion of the country's access to the Atlantic Ocean. Canadian territorial integrity would not be grossly violated by such a move. It is manifestly easier to build up than to tear apart.

Although the secession/partition examples proliferate, the insights we may garner from them into the Quebec situation are extremely limited. The crisis in the former Yugoslavia and the independence achieved by the Baltic States are often raised for the purposes of comparison, but, as the Grand Council of the Crees points out, "it would be imprudent to assume that the situation in the former Yugoslavia is in any way a prescription or precedent for secession in the context of Quebec." Furthermore, "there is no solid basis for a secessionist Quebec relying on the recent independence of the Baltic states as some form of relevant precedent."[1] The prime minister of Lithuania,

---

1 Grand Council of the Crees, *Sovereign Injustice* 108, 113.

Gediminas Vagnorius, on an official visit to Canada in 1991, stated: "The question of Lithuania or the Baltics could not be considered equal to the issue of Quebec. The situation in Lithuania is related to the decolonization process."[1] The predicament we find ourselves in today in Canada is, finally, unique in almost every aspect. We cannot resort to preexisting models in planning a course of action; we must depend upon our own collective imagination and ingenuity.

---

1 Warren Caragata, " 'No Comparison between Quebec and Baltics': Lithuanian PM Suggests Quebec Independence Is an Artificial Issue," *Gazette* 18 Apr. 1991: A1.

Conclusion

Partition validates and strengthens the principle of democratic debate. A free society draws its life blood from such debate, even though its evolution is often chaotic and inelegant. Partition is also a means by which federalist Quebecers can stave off the feelings of anxiety that currently afflict them. Positive action is the best antidote for despair. By pursuing the partitionist option, those determined to remain within the Canadian federation can continue to enjoy the protection of the Canadian Charter of Rights and Freedoms, protect their investments (financial and emotional, as well as investments of time and effort) in their homes and businesses, and hold on to the considerable benefits of Canadian citizenship.

Within a democratic nation, as various government administrations rise and fall, the state of the economy and the national mood can fluctuate significantly. But beneath the mutable surface of our political life is the underlying assumption that the mechanisms that guarantee our fundamental security will remain intact. The police will protect us. Our currency will retain value. We will have the right to work in another province and to move freely across all provincial borders. We will have medicare. We will only have to witness the invocation of martial law in the event of dire emergency. Our laws will remain in force.

Secession challenges this assumption. A UDI challenges the rule of law. Partitionists, and all advocates of Canadian unity, must put pressure on the federal government to enact contingency legislation now, so that if Quebec follows through with its threat to make a UDI, Canadians will not be left unprotected by the rule of law. The federal government must also be instructed to state clearly and unequivocally that it will not recognize a UDI, and that partition is a legitimate federalist recourse.

Most importantly, however, we must not lose sight of the fact that partition is plan B — a strong reaction to an extreme set of circumstances. If Quebec does succeed in illegally breaking away from the Canadian federation, each state will grab territory and attempt to assert effective control over it. No new borderlines will ever be drawn that will satisfy everyone. Conflict will be inevitable.